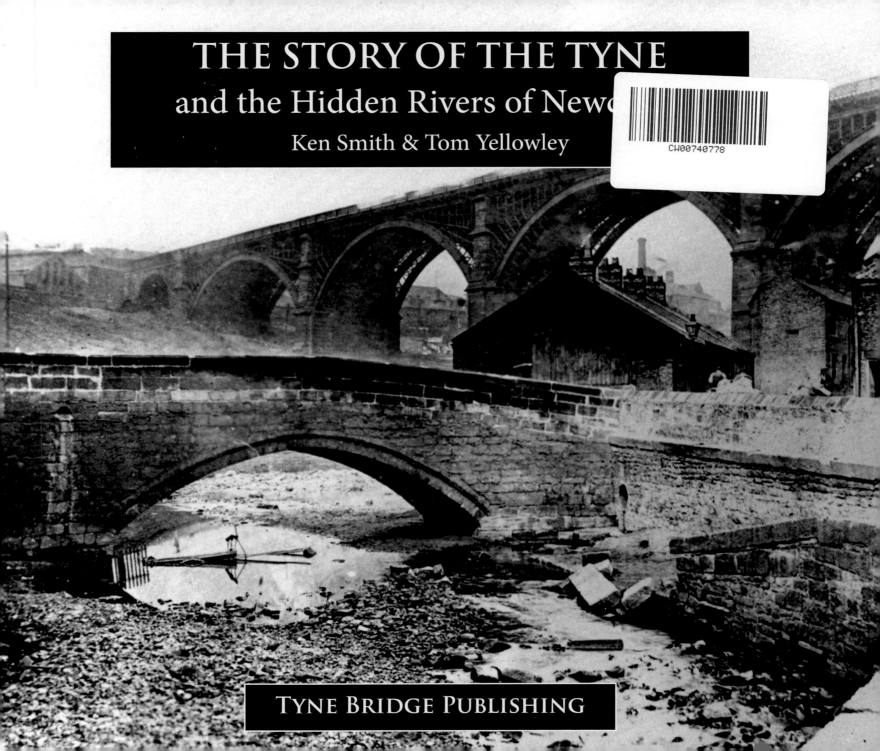

THE STORY OF THE TYNE
and the Hidden Rivers of New[castle]

Ken Smith & Tom Yellowley

CW00740778

TYNE BRIDGE PUBLISHING

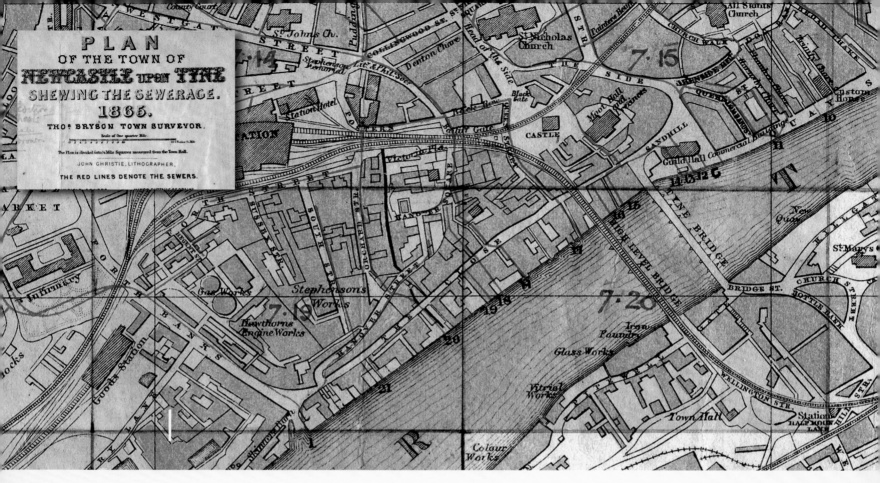

Contents Page: Bryson Plan of Newcastle 'Shewing the Sewerage' 1865.

Published by:
City of Newcastle Upon Tyne
Newcastle Libraries
Tyne Bridge Publishing, 2015
www.tynebridgepublishing.co.uk

Front Cover – View of the Tyne Bridge, November 1959, Tyne & Wear Archives & Museums.
Title Page – Crawford's Bridge over the Ouseburn 1910.
Contents Page: Bryson Plan of Newcastle 'Shewing the Sewerage' 1865.

Acknowledgements: The authors would like to thank the following for their kind help in the preparation of this book: David Hepworth, Tyne Bridge Publishing, Vanessa Histon, Alan Morgan, Jim Cuthbert, Ron French, Dick Keys, Stafford Linsley and the staff of Newcastle City Libraries.

Photographs: Dr. Tom Yellowley, David Hepworth, Newcastle Libraries, Tyne & Wear Museums and Archives.

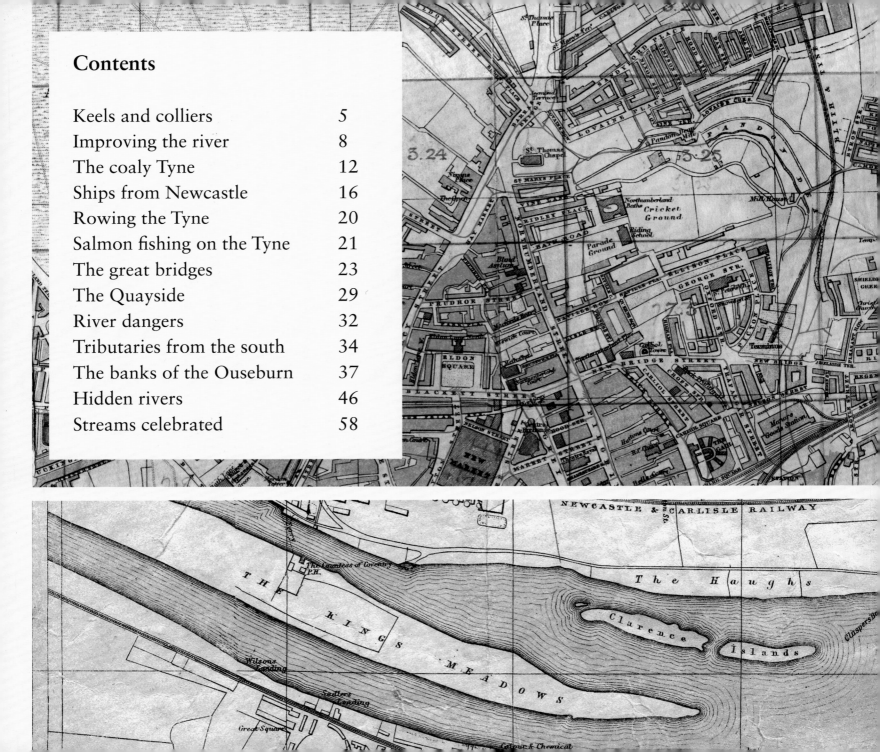

Contents

4

Newcastle's bustling Quayside in 1970

Keels and Colliers

For hundreds of years the River Tyne was a troublesome waterway to sail along because of its sand banks, shallows, tortuous bends and islands. Ships often found it difficult to navigate its waters up to Newcastle and were unable to sail further upstream than the town's quayside. The arches of the Old Tyne Bridge and its 18th century replacement bridge were too low to allow larger sailing vessels to pass further up river where most of the early coal pits were situated, and the water at this point was too shallow.

At low tide, ships that had reached Newcastle were frequently grounded on the sand of its quayside. It was sometimes possible to wade across the river at the point where the High Level Bridge was later built.

Yet despite this difficulty, the Tyne became of major importance to the North East and Britain as the result of the vast reserves of coal found in Northumberland and County Durham. From the 13th and 14th centuries onwards the coal was mined and exported from the region via the river in ever increasing quantities. That expansion of output continued until the early 20th century. Shipments of coal and coke from the Tyne reached their peak in 1923 when more than 21 million imperial tons left the river. An earlier peak of over 20 million tons had been achieved in 1911.

By the 16th and 17th centuries, craft had appeared that were able to navigate the tricky waterway loaded with the precious, dusty cargo and bring the coal down to the larger collier ships waiting in Shields Harbour at the mouth of the Tyne or in the lower reaches of the river below Newcastle bridge. These small boats were known as keels – small, distinctive vessels that were manned by equally distinctive

Boats near the Tyne Bridge, 1807.

5

crews, most of whom lived in the Sandgate district of Newcastle. During their heyday in the 17th and 18th centuries, keels were the most numerous craft passing Newcastle's Quayside. They numbered hundreds.

The keel was an oval-shaped, very broad-beamed boat with a flat bottom. It was generally about 40ft long and its open-topped oblong hold took up most of the space in the centre of the boat. When needed it was propelled by oars, the longest of which – known as a swape – was also used as a rudder. When conditions were favourable keels employed sail power using a single mast. However, the main motive force was provided by the tides. Long poles known as 'pouys' were used to move the craft away from the side of the shore or in other situations in shallow water.

The crew generally consisted of a skipper, two men – known as 'keel bullies' – and a boy, who was known as a 'pee dee'. The origin of the term 'pee dee' is a mystery, but it may have been a reference to the small size of a boy. In The *Making of the Tyne* (1895), R.W. Johnson points out that in his day Tyneside schoolboys called their marbles 'pee dees'.

After taking on their cargo at riverside loading quays known as staiths, the keelmen would use the ebb tide to drop down to the ships waiting at Shields Harbour or to vessels moored in the river below Newcastle Bridge. On reaching their destination, they would unload the coal by casting it up into the waiting ships using shovels. As can be imagined, casting up was an arduous task requiring great strength and endurance. The keelmen would then wait for the incoming tide to carry them back up river, often using sail power to assist their passage. The round trip might take 12 to 15 hours.

The Keelmen's Hospital on City Road in Newcastle stands as a testament to the altruism of these hardy workers. In 1697-99 they formed a charity to build the hospital, which opened in 1701 as a residential home for elderly, sick or infirm keelmen and their widows. It cost £2,000 and the working keelmen paid for it themselves (four pence per keel journey was deducted from their wages).

The staiths above Newcastle Bridge were generally referred to as 'spouts' after the chutes down which the coal tumbled into the keels. Sometimes the term 'dykes' was used for these loading points. During the 18th century most of the spouts became linked to the mines by horse-operated waggonways.

On the northern bank to the west of Newcastle town centre, during the 18th century there were spouts at Benwell, Elswick and Scotswood connected to Adair's Main,

The Keelmen's Hospital, c.1880.

Walbottle and Holywell Main collieries. By the early 19th century a spout had also been installed at Lemington which was linked to Wylam Colliery and there were several important loading points on the south side of the river.

Keels were the ideal solution to the problem of shallows, obstructions and problematic bends in the river as long as most of the pits were situated mainly up river to the west of Newcastle bridge.

However, by 1787 at least nine collieries had opened relatively near to the lower reaches below the bridge and were linked to the river by waggonways. The number of pits connected to the lower reaches increased during the early 1800s. Accordingly, there was an increase in collier ships sailing up river at high tide to receive coal directly into their holds at staiths in the lower reaches between Shields and Pelaw. These staiths sometimes had improved loading facilities with jetties that projected out into deeper water. Even at Shields, some direct loading staiths had been installed by 1771.

The keelmen realised that this direct loading was a threat to their livelihood. Strikes ensued, including a major stoppage in 1822 when they tried to prevent any coal from leaving the river. The blockade was broken by William Hedley, the viewer of Wylam Colliery, who mounted one of his pioneering steam locomotives on a keel and used the engine to drive paddle wheels. This improvised tug then towed a line of loaded keels from Lemington Staiths to Shields.

Yet as far as the future of shipping was concerned, the biggest issue was the poor state of the Tyne. Sand, gravel, chalk, flint and other material carried as ballast by colliers

The Tyne Bridge, c.1783. Note that the masts of the ships prevent them travelling west beyond the bridge.

and other ships was dumped at various points on the river's banks. Hills of ballast developed, but the material often slipped into the river, sometimes as the result of wind and rain. Adding to this problem, ships frequently discharged their ballast into the Tyne to avoid paying charges for unloading it on the shores. This practice led to the waterway becoming increasingly shallow and clogged.

By around 1850 the situation was in urgent need of remedy and by 1860 the river was said to be in the worst state it had ever been. Newcastle Corporation, the authority governing the port, faced constant criticism for allowing the waterway to deteriorate and for its failure to spend enough money to tackle the problem.

Improving the River

The Newcastle Corporation governed the Tyne until the advent of the Tyne Improvement Commission in 1850. Citing a series of royal charters over the centuries, the corporation had claimed complete control over trade and shipping. This led to disputes between Newcastle and other towns such as North Shields, South Shields and Gateshead.

Newcastle's jurisdiction over the waterway was from Sparrow Hawk, a sand bar at the mouth of the river near Tynemouth headland, to the tidal flow limit at Hedwin Streams, one and a half miles above Newburn, marked by the Tide Stone. Revenue derived from the various dues paid by port users, such as charges for dumping ballast, went to Newcastle, but improvements to the river were few.

It was the deterioration in the state of the waterway that led to the formation of the Tyne Improvement Commission. This body took over as the river conservator and representatives from the various Tyneside local authorities, including Newcastle, became members of the commission.

In 1845 a river police force was established. This had superseded Newcastle Corporation's water bailiff, previously known as the 'serjeant of the water', and his assistants who had enforced the town's control along the Tyne. These officials had been empowered to seize goods being traded by other towns on the river in defiance of Newcastle's control. Newcastle also had a river court and river jury to try any cases resulting from breaches of its charters.

Below: A view from the King's Meadows, an island in the Tyne. The ship in the background at the Elswick Yard is the Panther launched in June 1885.
Right: A work pass issued by the Tyne Improvement Commission, 1914.

From the middle of the 19th century onwards, steamships began replacing sailing vessels for the transport of North East coal to London, other areas of Britain and the world. Steam-driven vessels were faster, more reliable and could carry a greater quantity of coal than the sailing colliers, which were dependent on the vagaries of the wind and tides. Hand-in-hand with this development came the introduction of water ballast tanks. Solid ballast was no longer needed.

The advent of the steamship and increasing coal output meant a clear waterway was imperative for expansion of the port's trade. Accordingly, in 1861 the Tyne Improvement Commission launched a long-term programme of extensive dredging that deepened the channel. Sand and mud banks, shallows, islands and other obstructions to navigation were removed.

This work included the removal of a protruding 72ft high cliff known as Bill Point at Walker. Steering a vessel around this bluff had been a difficult task requiring great skill. Vessels approaching from opposite directions were unable to see each other because of the projecting cliff. To solve the problem, the headland was cut back by around 400ft and rock beneath the low water mark blasted away with dynamite. Further up river, King's Meadows Island and another island known as the Annie, both off the Elswick shore, were gradually dredged away.

King's Meadows covered around 30 acres and had a popular pub, the Countess of Coventry, whose landlady supplied the village of Elswick with milk from the cows she kept on the island. Horse races were held there and it was a prime spot from which to watch regattas. Patrons were rowed across from the mainland.

Construction work on embankments and piers at Newcastle Quayside.

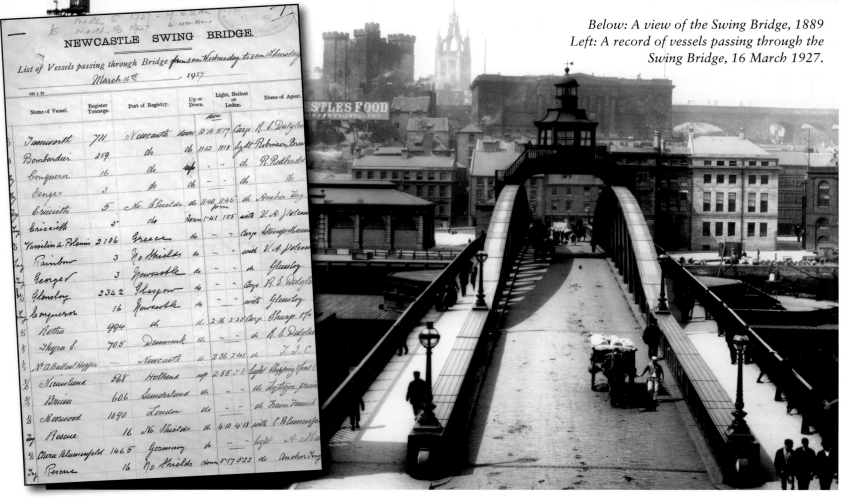

Below: A view of the Swing Bridge, 1889
Left: A record of vessels passing through the Swing Bridge, 16 March 1927.

In the first 20 years of operations the number of dredgers was increased from three to six and they were assisted by a fleet of steam tugs and hopper barges. By 1866, more than five million tons of material had been taken from the river bed and dumped out to sea.

The Tyne was widened and straightened as well as deepened. It was now much easier for ships to journey up river and load their cargo directly at the staiths. The need for keel boats steeply declined. They faded away during the second half of the 19th century.

The Tyne Improvement Commission and North Eastern Railway also built improved, larger staiths so that steamers could take on their cargoes quickly and efficiently. These included Tyne Dock, Northumberland Dock and Dunston Staiths.

In 1876, the new Swing Bridge, which replaced the 18th century bridge of low arches, was completed and this enabled larger vessels to sail up river from the centre of Newcastle. Ships could now reach the up-river staiths. The opening machinery and superstructure of the bridge had been built by Sir W.G. Armstrong and Company of Elswick in the West End of Newcastle.

By 1900, the most numerous ships passing Newcastle's Quayside were the steam colliers bound for or departing from staiths west of the Swing Bridge. The year 1929 witnessed 5,239 vessels pass through the bridge, the majority of them colliers. They took on their cargo at the large Dunston Staiths and at other staiths such as Derwenthaugh, Low Elswick, Stella and Lemington.

When a collier approached the bridge she would sound three blasts on her steam whistle. The bridge would answer with three blasts from its own siren and then, using its hydraulic machinery, swing open to allow the vessel through.

Steamships had now superseded sailing vessels as the carriers of black diamonds. By the 1890s a steamer could load 1,000 tons on the Tyne in four or five hours and complete the voyage to London and back in four days. They frequently made around 60 such voyages in one year. This was well beyond the ability of a sailing collier.

Steam and sail on the Quayside, 1880.

The Tyne from Dunston Staiths, c.1930.

The Coaly Tyne

Down river from the great bridges between Newcastle and Gateshead, the banks of the Tyne were, by 1900, crowded with shipyards, staiths and quays. Vessels of almost every description left the waterway for numerous destinations and ships entered the river with a wide range of cargoes.

Coal was overwhelmingly the greatest cargo carried from the Tyne. It went to London, the South Coast, and the near Continent and to ports throughout much of the world.

Ships coming into the river might be 'in ballast' – carrying only water in bottom-level tanks for stability, but otherwise empty. Unsurprisingly, they were visiting to load cargoes of coal.

Some vessels, however, brought imports before they took on the black diamonds. Timber from the Baltic for pit props and railway sleepers was a common inward cargo.

Before 1850 coal exports from the Tyne had grown to about five and a quarter million imperial tons a year, but between then and the early 1900s the shipments increased enormously.

In 1911 more than 20 million tons of coal and coke were carried away from the river. In 1913 exports again reached over 20 million tons. Although this figure fell during the First World War, shipments recovered afterwards, reaching a peak of more than 21 million tons in 1923. This total was never again matched or exceeded.

Below: Coal wagons are used to load a ship at Tyne Dock, 1900.
Right: 1889 ticket showing transfer of coal at Albert Edward Dock.

The booming trade in coal was greatly assisted by the Tyne Improvement Commission which made the river one of the best ports on the east coast. Dredging operations included the gradual removal of the treacherous Tyne Bar at the river mouth, and the deepening, widening and straightening of the waterway for a distance of around 14 miles inland from the North Sea.

As well as coal exports, the Tyne gained a well-deserved reputation as a port for bunkering. Ships seeking coal to refuel their engines could speedily and cheaply replenish their bunkers at staiths not far from the river mouth and so achieve a quick turn-around time at low cost.

Steam collier ships were attended to by shore-based workmen known as teemers and trimmers. The teemers carried out the actual loading of vessels, operating the equipment needed for this process. The trimmers, armed with shovels, would level out the coal in the holds, helping to ensure stability and 'knocking the top' off the black diamonds to enable the hatches to be closed.

One of the earliest loading methods was the waggon drop, a system in which a coal truck was lowered from the staith on to the deck of a ship. A door was then opened in the bottom of the waggon and the coal cascaded into the hold. Alternatively, a waggon would remain on a staith, the doors in its bottom were opened and the cargo allowed to stream down a spout (also sometimes known as a chute) into the ship. This gravity spout method eventually superseded the waggon drop.

During the early years of the 20th century electric conveyor belts were introduced for loading; an important advance in efficiency, particularly at high tides.

Above: A drawing of coal staiths by Thomas H. Hair, 1840.
Right: Coal conveyor belt on the south bank, 1974.

13

By 1925 there were six major coal-loading points on the Tyne. They were: Tyne Dock; Dunston Staiths and West Dunston Staiths, owned by the London and North Eastern Railway (formerly the North Eastern Railway); Northumberland Dock at Howdon and the adjacent Whitehill Point Staiths at North Shields, owned by the Tyne Improvement Commission; and Derwenthaugh Staiths, owned by the Consett Iron Company.

In addition, there was a considerable number of smaller staiths, often owned by the colliery companies, such as Harton Staiths at South Shields and those at Jarrow (Springwell Staiths), Hebburn, Pelaw Main, Blaydon (Priestman Staith), Heworth (Dean Primrose Staiths), Stella, Wallsend, Elswick and Lemington (Throckley Staiths).

One of the principal loading facilities was at Tyne Dock on the south bank, which, by 1925, had exported more coal than any other dock in the world. The grand total at this time was said to have exceeded 313 million tons. In 1908

7.5 million tons of County Durham coal and coke cascaded from its staiths into the holds of waiting ships.

This large dock, which opened in 1859, had four staiths, that enabled 16 vessels to load at the same time. There were 42 spouts and eight electric conveyor belts. Two or more spouts could be operated on one steamer simultaneously, thus achieving rapid loading.

1950s Staithsmen's tickets.

Wallsend riverside, 1910.

The London and North Eastern Railway Company declared in an advertisement of 1925: 'Tyne Dock has the reputation for giving the quickest despatch in the country for vessels taking coal.'

At Northumberland Dock (opened in 1857), on the north side of the river, there were eight staiths, four operated by coal companies of South-East Northumberland and four by the London and North Eastern Railway.

Also on the north side, on a bend in the river a little to the east of Northumberland Dock were the Whitehill Point Staiths. These were often used by bunkering ships, but also loaded colliers with their cargo. The facility featured three hydraulic lifts that could raise trucks up to 45ft above the jetties, allowing large ships to be loaded by electric conveyor belts no matter how high the tide. The Tyne was truly the river of coal, the bedrock on which the North East's population growth and industrial development was founded.

The Tyne's impressive protective North and South Piers were constructed at the river mouth. This project lasted many years. Work began on the North Pier at Tynemouth in 1854 but it was beset with problems, being breached by storms in 1867 and again, more seriously in 1897.

Afterwards, the pier was rebuilt in a straight line to make it stronger than the original curved design. The pier was finally completed in 1909. Work on the longer South Pier at South Shields also began in the same year. It was completed in 1895.

The North Pier was breached by a storm in 1897

Ships from Newcastle

Newcastle's great waterway was a river of shipbuilding as well as coal. The Swing Bridge had enabled Armstrong's company to open a shipyard at Elswick in 1884-85. The yard became famous for its warships, particularly its fast cruisers, which were built for the navies of many countries, including Japan, China, Argentina, Brazil and Chile. The Imperial Japanese Navy was a particularly valued customer. Nine warships were completed for Japan between 1893 and 1906. They included such impressive vessels as the cruisers *Asama*, *Iwate*, *Idzumo*, *Tokiwa* and *Yoshino*, and the battleships *Hatsuse*, *Yashima* and *Kashima*.

Ships were also constructed at Elswick for Britain's Royal Navy. The First World War battleships HMS *Agincourt* and HMS *Canada* were among the largest vessels to be launched at the yard and to pass down river through the open Swing Bridge. These huge warships signalled a change of location. Armstrong Whitworth, as the company was known from 1897, realised that the increasing size of new ships meant that sooner or later they would be unable to fit through the bridge's channels. A new yard down river was needed.

Accordingly, construction of the Naval Yard at Walker in the East End of Newcastle began around 1910 – 1911. The scheme involved extensive dredging of the river. HMS *Agincourt* and HMS *Canada* were launched in 1913 at Elswick but moved down river to be fitted out at the new yard.

The first major vessel launched at the Walker Naval Yard was the battleship HMS *Malaya*, completed in early 1916. The yard went on to build many other significant vessels, including the pioneering aircraft carrier HMS *Furious* (completed 1917), the Second World War battleship HMS *King George V* (1940) and the passenger liners *Mongolia* (1923), *Gripsholm* (1925), *Monarch of Bermuda* (1931), *Ocean Monarch* (1951), *Empress of England* (1956) and *Empress of Canada* (1961).

Armstrong Whitworth's Low Walker Yard, which had been founded by Aberdonian Charles Mitchell in 1852 – 1853, was a short distance down river from the Naval Yard. The Low Walker Yard's many vessels included icebreakers for Russia such as the *Yermak* (1899) and the pioneering oil tanker *Gluckauf* (1886). Numerous other tankers were built at this yard, and more than 90 vessels of various types were completed for Russia.

Further down river, but still at Low Walker, was the location of a shipyard founded by John Coutts in around 1842. Coutts was one of the pioneers of iron shipbuilding on the Tyne. Later, the site became the Neptune Yard of John Wigham Richardson. Among Neptune's vessels was the *Colonia* (1902), which was the first of 24 cableships launched at the yard to lay and repair telegraph or telephone cables. Other significant vessels included the *Hornby Grange* (1890), one of the world's first large refrigerated cargo ships. Merchant vessels were very much the order of the day. Wigham Richardson was a Quaker and while he headed the firm the Neptune Yard never built a warship.

Japanese warships built on the Tyne at the Elswick Yard of Armstrong, Whitworth and Co:

Top: Under tow, Iwate, a cruiser launched 23 March 1900. Sunk by US carrier aircraft near Kure in 1945.

Centre: Tatsuta, a Japanese torpedo boat destroyer at full speed. Made at Armstrong Whitworth in 1918 and renamed Nagaura Maru in 1926.

Bottom right: Yoshino, a cruiser launched in 1893. Sank off Liao-Tung Peninsula after a collision with the Kasugo.

Bottom left: Drawing of Kashima, a First Class Battleship also built at the Elswick Yard, launched on 22 March 1905. Broken up in 1923–24.

Clockwise from top left: 1) The Blenheim built at St. Peter's Yard, launched 18 July 1848. At 1,489 tons the largest merchant ship in Europe at the time. 2) Gripsholm, Swedish passenger liner 1925, Armstrong Yard, Walker. 3) RMS Empress of England was an ocean liner built in 1956-1957 by Vickers-Armstrongs for the Canadian Pacific Line. The ship was launched in 1956 and she undertook her maiden voyage in 1957. 4) The launch of Yermack in 1898, used as a Russian ice-breaker until 1965.

Shipbuilding had existed in Newcastle long before the advent of iron and, later, steel vessels. Wooden sailing vessels were launched on the North Shore, immediately to the west of the mouth of the Ouseburn, and at St Peter's to the east. Shipbuilding seems to have been well-established by the 17th century when a shipwrights' guild was formed in Newcastle. Shipwrights mended vessels that entered the river to collect coal or other cargoes and they also had the skills to build ships.

The shipbuilding yard of William Rowe at St Peter's constructed a number of substantially sized ocean-going vessels between 1756 and 1810. Perhaps the most impressive was the 150ft long *Bucephalus*, a 32 gun frigate built for the Royal Navy, which was launched in 1808.

This yard was taken over by Alderman Thomas Smith, a rope manufacturer, and his sons William and Thomas, in 1810. Following his death his sons carried on the business. The firm, which became known as T&W Smith, launched mainly wooden vessels at the yard until the 1860s. From 1828 to 1861 the output at St Peter's included large sailing ships known as East Indiamen, intended, as their name implied, for trade to India and the Far East. The first was the *Duke of Roxburghe* in 1828. Others included the *Duke of Northumberland* (1831), the *Ellenborough* (1842), the *Gloriana* (1843) and the *Hotspur* (1851). In 1846-48, T&W Smith completed their largest East Indiamen, the *Marlborough* and the *Blenheim*.

Also launched at St Peter's was the 50-gun warship *Carlo Alberto*, completed for the Sardinian government in 1853. It was reported that the launch of this vessel was watched by 40,000 people. She was the largest ship to be built on the Tyne at that date. Today the site of the yard is covered by the St Peter's housing estate and marina.

Ship launches were not the only events that drew the crowds to the river's banks. Every year on Ascension Day during the early 19th century, the Mayor of Newcastle, other civic dignitaries, the Master and Brethren of Trinity House in Newcastle and representatives of the town's trade and craft guilds, had taken part in a procession of brightly decorated barges along the river to emphasise Newcastle's jurisdiction over the Tyne.

Known as Barge Day, this ritual tour of inspection of the waterway began with the Mayor's barge and accompanying vessels leaving the quay by the town's 17th century Mansion House in The Close and proceeding down river to Sparrow Hawk. The barges would then be rowed back upstream to Hedwin Streams. Newcastle's authority over the river was proclaimed at each of these destinations. Stops for refreshments were made at the Mansion House and King's Meadows Island.

Barge Day, 25 May 1844 (TWAM).

The foundation of the Tyne Improvement Commission in 1850 did not stop this colourful event, although during the second half of the 19th century it was held every five years instead of annually. The last Barge Day took place in 1901.

Rowing on the Tyne

The 19th century also witnessed the emergence of rowing as a popular sport on the Tyne. Famed oarsmen such as Harry Clasper, Bob Chambers and James Renforth were the toast of the river in mid-Victorian times and their exploits attracted much larger crowds to the river's banks than Barge Day.

Harry Clasper, who was born at Dunston on the south bank, won the single sculls race at the Durham Regatta in 1842, but he was to achieve his greatest renown rowing in fours races. However, he and his crew failed to beat a London crew in a fours race on the Tyne from Newcastle's 18th century Bridge to Lemington in the same year. There was great disappointment for the huge crowds who had turned up on the riverbank to cheer the Tyneside rowers on.

Clasper realised that the London crew had used a much lighter boat that had given them an undoubted advantage. Accordingly, he improved the design of the boats he used and made them lighter. In 1845, he and his men from the Tyne travelled to London and won the Champion Fours at the Thames Regatta. They went on to win this event six more times.

Harry Clasper died in 1870, aged 58. The funeral procession was watched by many thousands. A boat took his body up river from Newcastle for burial in St Mary's Churchyard, Whickham.

'Honest' Bob Chambers, from St Anthony's, Walker, became World Sculling Champion in 1859 when he raced against London rival Tom White. The contest took place on the Tyne from the High Level Bridge to Scotswood Suspension Bridge. In a controversial incident, Chambers found himself in collison with a keel and his opponent pulled away to take what seemed to be an unassailable lead. Despite this major setback, Chambers closed the gap

Above right: Empire Rowing Club, Gateshead, c. 1900.
Below right: Harry Clasper shown in Illustrated Sporting News, 12 July 1862.

between himself and his opponent and won the race. Chambers went on to defend his title successfully in 1863. Sadly, 'Honest' Bob died of TB at the age of 37 in 1868. He is buried in Walker Cemetery.

James Renforth, who was born in Gateshead, was another superb rower. He took the World Sculling Championship on the Thames in 1868. Like Clasper, he also competed in fours races. Renforth and his crew became the World Champion Fours when they competed on the St Lawrence River in Canada in 1870. The following year, however, tragedy struck when he was suddenly taken ill while he and his crew were rowing in defence of the championship, again in Canada. He passed away in the arms of crew member and friend Henry Kelly, the man Renforth had beaten in the world sculling event in 1868. Renforth was only 29. His grave is in Gateshead Cemetery and there is a statue of him dying in the arms of Kelly outside the Shipley Art Gallery, Gateshead.

Salmon fishing on the Tyne

Today, the River Tyne has been cleaned of its former industrial pollution and salmon have returned to its waters. During the 18th century, huge catches of salmon were made in the river. Early 19th century historian Eneas Mackenzie tells us that in ancient times the fisheries of the Tyne were of great importance.

Salmon were so plentiful that apprentices refused to eat the fish more than twice a week! Mackenzie states that more the 2,400 salmon were taken in the Tyne on 12 June 1755, and on 20 June 1758, over 2,000 were caught. One salmon, taken on 28 May 1760, weighed an impressive 54 pounds. On 6 August 1761, around 260 salmon were caught at Newburn.

Long abandoned wherries on the Tyne near Newburn.

The Great Bridges

Eleven bridges span the Tyne between Newburn and the centre of Newcastle. Seven of the most impressive are built close together, taking trains, vehicles and pedestrians into the heart of the city. The most westerly crossing, however, is several miles from the centre. This is Newburn Road Bridge, completed in 1893. It is a steel lattice structure supported by piers of wrought iron and concrete.

Moving eastwards, the next crossing is the modern Blaydon Bridge, completed in 1990. The opening ceremony was performed by the Queen in December of that year. This road bridge carries the Newcastle and Gateshead Western Bypass.

Further down river, the disused Scotswood Rail Bridge, which opened in 1871, stands as a somewhat sad reminder that in former years the Newcastle and Carlisle Railway crossed the river at this point. Two other rail bridges preceded the present structure, the earliest of which was built in 1839. It was destroyed by fire.

A short distance to the east comes the steel, twin-arch Scotswood Road Bridge, opened in 1967 and designed by Mott, Hay & Anderson. This crossing replaced a fine suspension bridge that dated to 1831 and had been designed by renowned Newcastle architects John and Benjamin Green.

About a mile eastwards stands the slender, concrete Redheugh Bridge, completed in 1983, and designed by Mott, Hay & Anderson in cooperation with Tyne and Wear County Council. Hidden in the bridge structure are ducts that carry gas, electricity, water and telephone cables. This bridge replaced two earlier structures, the first of which was opened in 1871 and the second in 1901.

Only a short distance down river from the Redheugh, the Queen Elizabeth II Bridge carries the Tyne and Wear Metro rail line. Designed by W.A. Fairhurst & Partners, it is of steel construction and was built in prefabricated sections. The crossing was opened by the Queen in 1981.

Further eastwards, and again only a short distance away, the King Edward VII Bridge brings the main East Coast rail line into Newcastle Central Station from London, York, Darlington and Durham. The King Edward VII Bridge was designed by Charles Augustus Harrison, a chief engineer with the North Eastern Railway. It was completed in 1906. Appropriately, the opening ceremony was performed by Edward VII in July of that year. This magnificent structure features steel lattice girders and is supported by granite piers. The bridge carries four tracks. Its deck towers around 83ft above the high water mark.

Down river from the King Edward, comes a great masterpiece of civil engineering, the magnificent High Level Bridge with its two decks, the upper one for rail traffic and the lower for road vehicles and pedestrians. This was the first bridge to bring the railway line from the South across the Tyne into Newcastle. It was designed by famous Tyneside civil, locomotive and railway engineer Robert Stephenson, son of steam locomotive pioneer George Stephenson. Both were born on the banks of the river.

Working plans for the bridge were drawn up by Thomas Elliot Harrison, whose nephew Charles Augustus Harrison designed the King Edward VII Bridge. The High Level Bridge was completed in 1849.

Left top: A view showing the High Level Bridge and 18th Century Tyne Bridge, taken for the Tyne Improvement Commission by the pioneer photographer Thomas Worden in 1865 (Port of Tyne/TWAM).
Left bottom: A steam train rattles over the High Level Bridge, 1925.

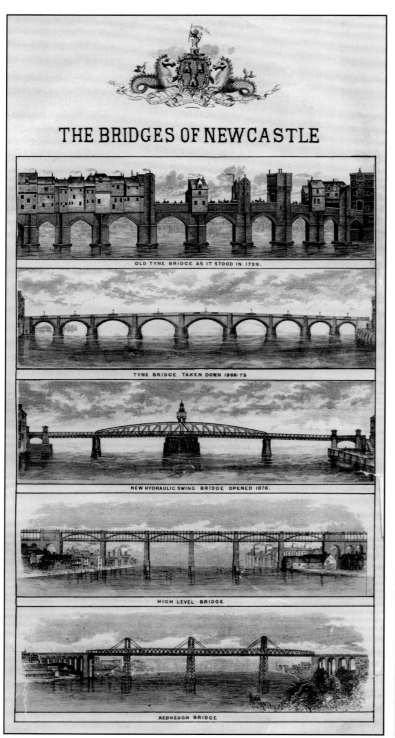

THE BRIDGES OF NEWCASTLE

OLD TYNE BRIDGE AS IT STOOD IN 1739.

TYNE BRIDGE TAKEN DOWN 1866-75

NEW HYDRAULIC SWING BRIDGE OPENED 1876.

HIGH LEVEL BRIDGE

REDHEUGH BRIDGE

DORMAN. LONG & C? LTD

Area XX.

Before Presentation. Row 6 Seat 7

After Presentation. Row DD Seat 1

45

OPENING OF NEW TYNE BRIDGE
by
H.M. THE KING
on
WEDNESDAY, OCTOBER 10th, 1928.

ADMIT Mr Albert Blacklock

ENTER by the Newcastle Approach. Please bring this card
with you and be in your position by 10-45 a.m.

Near left: The Tyne Bridge under construction, February 1928. Far left: From an engraving of the bridges of Newcastle.
Inset left: Ticket to the opening of the New Tyne Bridge, 10 October 1928
Above clockwise from top left: 1) Sunset behind the Tyne 'riverscape'. 2) The King Edward VII Bridge. 3) The High Level Bridge restored and reopened in 2008. 4) 20 November 2000 the huge Dutch crane, Asian Hercules II lowers the Gatehead Millennium Bridge into place.

Queen Victoria was among the first to use the High Level Bridge. Her train stopped on the bridge as she journeyed from Scotland to the South of England in September of that year. This great cast and wrought iron structure is supported by masonry piers on huge timber piles. Its lower deck is suspended around 82ft above high water.

The next crossing down river, only a very short distance away, is the Swing Bridge of 1876. Its iron superstructure and hydraulic opening machinery were, as outlined earlier, built by Sir W.G. Armstrong & Company of Elswick, and the supporting stone piers and abutments by the Tyne Improvement Commission. Today, the bridge is still operated by hydraulic power, although since 1959 electric pumps have replaced those operated by steam.

It is believed by some that the Swing Bridge was built on the approximate line of the Roman bridge. However, there is no definite proof of this. Two Roman stone altars, to the gods Neptune and Oceanus, were found in the river during the 19th century. They are believed to have stood on the Roman bridge, but the exact position of the crossing is unknown. The altars are today on display in The Great North Museum at Barras Bridge, Newcastle.

Next in this splendid line-up of crossings comes the famed Tyne Bridge, another masterpiece, completed in 1928 and officially opened by King George V in October of that year. It was designed by Mott, Hay and Anderson and built by Dorman, Long of Middlesbrough. The road deck of this mighty twin-arch steel crossing is suspended 84ft above high water. At low water, the distance is nearly 100ft. The ends of the bridge are adorned by twin Cornish granite towers.

Mott, Hay & Anderson also designed the giant Sydney Harbour Bridge in Australia and the Tyne Bridge was based on the Sydney design. Although work on building the Sydney Harbour crossing began around eight months before work on the Tyne Bridge, the Tyne crossing was completed first. The much larger Sydney bridge took over three years longer to finish and was not opened until 1932.

The last bridge down river, around ten miles from the

Above: The Swing Bridge and Tuxedo Royale, early 1990s.
Right: The Old Tyne Bridge damaged in the great flood of 1771.

North Sea, is the elegantly impressive Gateshead Millennium Bridge. It is sometimes referred to as the 'Blinking Eye' because of its ability to open by tilting to let ships and boats pass through. The structure features two steel arches, one carrying a deck for walkers and cyclists. Suspension cables run between the arches. The extraordinary and highly original design was by Gifford & Partners and Wilkinson Eyre Architects. The Gateshead Millennium Bridge was completed in 2001, the official opening ceremony being performed by the Queen in May the following year. It is perhaps at its most impressive at night when illuminated by coloured lighting.

The earliest bridge across the Tyne – known as Pons Aelius – was built by the Romans in around 122 AD, although it is not certain how long this crossing survived after the Roman withdrawal from Britain. The Old Tyne Bridge dated back to medieval times and is believed to have been built around 1250. This stone structure may have replaced an 11th or 12th century bridge, said to have been destroyed by fire in around 1248. There is, however, no clear evidence that this earlier medieval crossing existed, but if it did it may have incorporated elements of the former Roman bridge.

The Tyne Bridge of around 1250 – later referred to as the Old Tyne Bridge – was lined with shops and houses on the side nearest Gateshead and there was a chapel dedicated to St Thomas the Martyr (Thomas Becket) at its Newcastle end. Two gateway towers were built on the bridge, one of these close to the Gateshead end and the other between the third and fourth arches from the Newcastle bank. The Newcastle tower was used for a number of years as a prison.

Other features of the bridge included a chapel and hermitage for a priest who was left six marks a year by Newcastle mayor and wealthy merchant Roger Thornton to say prayers for the latter's soul. Thornton died in 1429. The Blue Stone was positioned on the bridge to mark the boundary between Newcastle and Gateshead. This stone is today displayed in Newcastle Keep.

The Tyne from Gateshead Millennium Bridge, 2015.

Perhaps the most impressive sight on the Old Tyne Bridge was the entry into Newcastle of Princess Margaret, daughter of Henry VII, in 1503. She was on her way to marry James IV of Scotland. Accompanied by a sumptuously dressed train of nobles, the princess was met on the bridge by the Mayor and Aldermen on foot.

Prominent among Margaret's retinue was the mounted Earl of Northumberland, who was dressed in gold, crimson and purple. He was followed by footmen in the same colours and riders in gold jackets. The mayor then mounted his horse and led the royal procession into Newcastle. Children on the gateway tower on the northern side of the bridge sang hymns and played musical instruments to welcome the royal guest. Princess Margaret stayed the night at the house of the Austin Friars at Manors. The King of Scotland who became her husband lost his life at the Battle of Flodden in 1513.

A curious story told about the Old Tyne Bridge concerns a ring. Around 1559, a merchant and alderman, known as Mr Anderson, is said to have been fingering the ring when he accidentally dropped it from the bridge into the river. He had been talking to a friend at the time. They may have been leaning over the parapet as they conversed. Some considerable time afterwards, one of Mr Anderson's servants bought a fish – possibly a salmon – in a Newcastle market and the ring was found inside the fish. As late 18th century historian John Brand puts it, the ring was 'most unexpectedly restored to its owner'.

The Old Tyne Bridge lasted for over 500 years, but in 1339 it was badly damaged by a flood and 120 people drowned. Despite this disaster, it survived and was repaired. In 1636, a gateway tower, known as the Magazine Gate, was built at the northern end of the bridge. This was probably because an earlier gateway, known as the Bridge End Gate, had fallen into decay and had been demolished.

During the Cromwellian period of the 17th century the arms of the Commonwealth were positioned on the Magazine Gate, but following the restoration of the monarchy in 1660 they were replaced with the royal arms and a statue of Charles II, accompanied by the motto (in latin): 'The coming of the King is the comfort of the people.'

The end for the old bridge came in 1771 when a major flood swept large sections of it away, including some of the shops and houses. Five people were drowned and two were reported to have died afterwards of 'fright'. The structure

was beyond repair. Its replacement, a stone bridge of nine low arches, was opened in 1781. The Blue Stone was rescued and re-erected on the new bridge.

The new crossing was jointly built by Newcastle Corporation and the Bishop of Durham, who were responsible for constructing their respective sections of the bridge. According to Brand, in 1774 a quarry was opened at Elswick to extract the stone needed to build Newcastle's section. Stone was also obtained from another quarry, down river at St Anthony's. The Bishop got his stone from a quarry at Oakwell Gate, Gateshead. The resulting bridge was demolished after 95 years of service and replaced by the Swing Bridge in 1876.

The Quayside

Coal was the main commodity exported from the Tyne but not the only one. For example, grindstones from the quarries of the Newcastle and Gateshead areas were shipped out from the river for hundreds of years to destinations worldwide. These stones were used to sharpen edge tools or as millstones to grind corn. Wool and leather were also among the earliest exports.

From medieval times onwards ships loaded or unloaded a wide variety of cargoes at Newcastle's Quayside. A fish market also developed by the quay, with small boats sailing right into the heart of the town to sell their catches.

The Quayside district today is the final result of a process of reclamation over the centuries. The shore of the Tyne along this stretch was moved forward into the river by infilling with ships' ballast (particularly flint), refuse and other material, narrowing the area uncovered at low tide. Dredging during the second half of the 19th century provided permanent deep water right up to the quay.

After completion of this dredging, however, it was found that the deeper river was endangering the foundations of the old quay, which was built of stone on timber piles. This situation caused subsidence in one or two places. Newcastle Corporation therefore decided to build a new quay, completed in around 1870, stretching from the Swing Bridge to the mouth of the Ouseburn. The new structure was based on cast-iron cylinders filled with concrete and faced with granite. The cost was £500,000, an enormous sum in Victorian times.

By the late 19th century, the numerous cargoes landed on the Quayside included huge quantities of foodstuffs, such as fruit, potatoes, cheese, eggs, butter, flour, bacon and lard. Livestock, including cattle, was also imported.

In 1870, a goods railway opened linking the main North East line with the Quayside. A tunnel with a very steep gradient carried the track on a curving route between the quay and sidings in the vicinity of New Bridge Street and Trafalgar Street in the Manors area. It was not an easy track to operate and specially adapted electric locomotives were later provided to better handle the steep slope. Despite this difficulty, the line survived until 1969.

During the late 19th and early 20th centuries, a multitude of shipping lines were using the Tyne, with services to and from numerous overseas countries, including Europe, the Mediterranean, North and South America, Africa and the Far East. These companies had agents' offices in central Newcastle, some near the Quayside, including Maritime Buildings in King Street, Milburn House near the top of the Side, Moor Buildings in Pilgrim Street and the Sun Insurance Building in Collingwood Street. Ships also departed for British destinations, including London, Hull, Aberdeen and Leith. Destinations were indicated by the names of the wharfs that lined the Quayside. They included the Aberdeen Wharf by the Guildhall, the Hull Wharf, Leith Wharf, the Antwerp, Hamburg and Rotterdam Wharf, and the Malmo Wharf. Among the passenger services were those provided by the Tyne Steam Shipping Company, later known as the Tyne-Tees Steam Shipping Company. They ran passenger ferries between Newcastle and London and carried travellers to destinations on the Continent.

In 1930, a total of 24 berths were available for visiting ships along 5,955ft of quay, backed by storage sheds or warehouses. Vessels were served by seven travelling cranes, five operated by steam and two by electricity. In addition, there was a fixed electric crane capable of lifting up to 65 imperial tons. As well as the stretch between the Swing Bridge and the Ouseburn, the quay included an extension immediately to the east of the Ouseburn at St Lawrence. A further extension of the quay at St Lawrence was built during the later 1930s. Meanwhile, the work of the Tyne Improvement Commission had continued. By the end of 1933, its dredgers had taken more than 160 million tons of material from the river bed.

A short distance to the west of the High Level Bridge, the Phoenix Flour Mill stood in the Close. Opened in 1855, the mill was taken over by Spillers in 1896. The company extended the premises so that they stretched from the site of the old Mansion House to the line of the old Town Walls. The tall wheat silos became a prominent feature of the Close. The company had its own steamship, the Harvest Queen, which brought wheat to a spacious wharf in front of the mill.

In 1938, however, Spillers moved down river to the new Tyne Mill at the eastern end of the Quayside extension at St Lawrence. It was the tallest milling building in the world at the time and featured a flour mill and giant silo capable of storing 34,000 tons of grain.

NESTLE'S FOOD
FOR INFANTS & INVALIDS

Quayside c.1893

Spillers Wharf, still active in 1992.

A deep water berth was provided for ships to moor alongside and discharge their cargoes. Equally imposing was the eight-storey Grain and General Warehouse, which, for many years, dominated the main stretch of the Quayside next to the Sandgate district. Fitted with elevators, the building was modelled on an American prototype. By the 1890s, cargoes received at this giant warehouse included wheat from San Francisco, other produce from New York and mutton from South America and New Zealand.

River Dangers

The Tyne has always been a dangerous river, with its sweeping tidal pull, strong currents and eddies. Historian Eneas Mackenzie, writing in the early 19th century, tells us that accidents and loss of life were frequent. During the 12 months preceding Michaelmas 1827,

River Police Station, 1906

Newcastle Corporation paid £15.15 shillings for the recovery from the river of 25 bodies. Mackenzie states that a chain had recently been placed along the town's Quayside to prevent accidents after sunset.

John Dixon, a Newcastle surgeon, had 'restored to life persons who would otherwise have perished'. In 1819, he recovered a man who had been 25 minutes in the water. In the same year, he resuscitated the mate of a Scottish vessel who had been in the water for 20 minutes. In 1820, Dixon revived – 'after some hours' exertion' – a boy who had fallen in the river.

Another life saver was Peter Gibson, a shoemaker of Dean Street, Newcastle, who was said to be a strong swimmer. He rescued several people from the river, including two men and a woman. One of them had fallen into the water on a dark winter night.

Many people who fell into the Tyne were not so lucky. Following the establishment of the River Police, grappling irons for the recovery of dead bodies were kept in a building known as the Dead House, situated almost immediately to the east of the mouth of the Ouseburn. This house also served as a morgue for the bodies. The River Police station was in the same building

The Dead House at St. Lawrence, 1879.

Tributaries from the south

Entering the Tyne from the south are the tributaries Don, Team and Derwent.

The River Don flows into the Tyne next to the site of Jarrow Slake, which was an extensive area of mudflats, covered at high water. The area has now been filled in and covered over to form the Tyne Car Terminal.

The Slake, or 'Slack' as it was sometimes called, featured timber ponds where imported wood was stored for seasoning in the tidal waters.

Shortly before reaching the Tyne the Don flows past the site of the Jarrow monastery where the Venerable Bede (c.672-735) lived as a monk and became England's first historian. A brilliant academic of great diligence and ability, he wrote the *Ecclesiastical History of the English People*, illuminating for posterity the Dark Ages following the end of Roman rule in Britain.

The River Team enters the Tyne on the western side of Gateshead, next to Dunston Staiths. Its lower reaches were once at the centre of a mining area. Dunston Colliery was on the western side of the Team. The pit opened in 1875 and closed in 1947. On the eastern side of this small tributary was Redheugh Colliery, which opened in 1872 and lasted until 1927. These mines were only a short distance from the confluence with the Tyne.

A little further to the south, on the western bank of the Team, was Norwood Cokeworks, which dated to 1912. Coke, a smokeless fuel, was produced by baking coal to remove some of its elements, principally sulphur, to make it suitable for industrial processes such as malting and smelting. The Norwood site was closed in the 1980s.

The River Derwent meets the Tyne at Derwenthaugh, where important staiths of the Consett Iron Company were situated. It was in nearby Winlaton village (c.1691-92) that Ambrose Crowley set up one of the earliest iron works in the North-East. The works produced small tools such as saws, chisels and hammers. He also opened sister works at Winlaton Mill in the Derwent Valley and later operated a third works at Swalwell. The workforces at these two sites turned out heavier products such as anchors, pumps and chains.

The site of Crowley's Winlaton Mill Iron Works was close to the location of the Derwenthaugh Cokeworks, which were opened in 1928, a little to the south of the Derwent's confluence with the Tyne. The cokeworks were linked to Derwenthaugh Staiths by rail. The plant closed in 1986 and the land was redeveloped as a park.

The confluence of the Rivers Derwent and Tyne at Derwenthaugh Viaduct, 1940.

Jarrow Slake, 1975.

Dunston Staiths.

JESMOND DENE.

Stepping Stones, Jesmond Dene, Newcastle-on-Tyne.

The Brash Series.

The Banks of the Ouseburn

The most prominent of four main tributaries that run through Newcastle into the Tyne is the Ouseburn. Unlike the other three watercourses, it is only culverted for a relatively short stretch. The main source of the Ouseburn is in a stream originating to the north west of the city at Callerton Pond. From Callerton, the burn continues eastwards and is joined by another stream that has its source in the Black Callerton area.

The burn then runs to Woolsington, passing under the main road in the village, before being joined by another brook from the direction of Newcastle Airport. It continues eastwards and crosses Brunton Lane, passing to the north of Fawdon. It then journeys to Brunton Park, along the edge of the City of Newcastle Golf Club course and reaches the Great North Road at Gosforth. It flows under this road at the Three Mile Bridge and then under the White Bridge to Dentsmires Bridge and Gosforth Golf Course. After reaching Salters Bridge, the burn continues to South Gosforth, passing the site of the former Gosforth Colliery a short distance before it reaches Haddricks Mill Bridge, near the Victory Public House.

Gosforth Colliery, which was on the eastern side of the burn, was opened in 1829. Sinking had begun in 1825 and the coal was won on January 31, 1829. The event was celebrated on February 6 by the holding of an underground ball, almost 1,100 feet below the surface. The reported 200 to 300 men and women who descended included sinkers and their wives and sweethearts. They danced in a 'ballroom' space 15ft wide and 48ft high which had been brilliantly lit by numerous lamps and candles. Flagstones were laid down to provide a relatively smooth floor. Music was provided by the Coxlodge Band. Many of the dancers obtained pieces of coal as mementoes of the occasion.

After passing Haddricks Mill Bridge, the Ouseburn enters Jesmond Dene, a beautiful, wooded gorge with precipitous, rocky sides. The word 'dene' implies a steep-sided, narrow valley. The stream passes the site of the now vanished Haddricks Mill, which appears in records as early as 1539. A Victorian map indicates that this water-driven mill was still grinding corn in around 1862.

Much of Jesmond Dene has been a public park since the late 19th century thanks to the benevolence of one man. In 1883, it was given to Newcastle Corporation by industrialist and inventor Sir William Armstrong of Cragside for the enjoyment of the city's people. The dene was officially opened to the public in 1884 by the Prince and Princess of Wales (later King Edward VII and Queen Alexandra), who marked the occasion by planting a turkey oak close to the Banqueting Hall on the western bank of the valley. The hall had been built by Armstrong to entertain customers of his Elswick Works, Newcastle, which during the 19th century grew into a major engineering, shipbuilding and armaments concern. As well as the dene, Armstrong also gave the Banqueting Hall to the corporation. It survives to this day.

The wealthy industrialist owned a house, known as Jesmond Dean, a short distance to the west of the valley and not far from the Banqueting Hall. To provide easy access for himself, his guests and servants, a tunnel was built from his home, running beneath Jesmond Dene Road, to the hall.

Left: Early 1900s postcards of Jesmond Dene.
Bottom Right: St Mary's Well, 1975, but not the original of medieval times.

A little to the south of the site of Armstrong's home, which was demolished in the 1930s, stand the ruins of St Mary's Chapel. The chapel became a place of pilgrimage during the Medieval period and parts of the ruins date to the 12th century. The building is close to Reid Park Road and Jesmond Dene Road. Pilgrims came to Newcastle from all over Britain to visit the chapel, the shrine of Our Lady of Jesmond. Miracles were said to have occurred in the vicinity and were linked to a spring known as St Mary's Well. This is likely to have been near one of the walls of the chapel.

Some confusion may have been caused by the fact that there is another spring named St Mary's Well, featuring a disused bathing pool, a short distance to the west of the ruins. However, this has been dated to no earlier than the 17th century.

Newcastle historian Henry Bourne, writing in the early 18th century, seems to be referring to this well when he states: 'St Mary's Well in this village (Jesmond), which is said to have had as many steps down to it as there are articles of the creed, was lately enclosed by Mr Coulson for a bathing place, which no sooner done than the water left it.' He added, with a touch of humour: 'The well was always esteemed of more sanctity than common wells, and therefore the failing of the water could be looked upon as nothing less than a just revenge for so great a profanation. But alas! The miracle's at an end for the water returned a while ago in as great abundance as ever.'

There is a third spring behind the gate house of Jesmond Grove, a large house demolished in 1927. A tunnel was excavated beneath Jesmond Dene Road to allow residents of Jesmond Dene Terrace to draw water from this well.

The Ouseburn flows through the dene over several weirs, beside sandstone bluffs, and then cascades over a large rocky outcrop to form an impressive waterfall, close to the ruins of the Old Mill. There is a fine view of the waterfall from the single-arch stone footbridge.

The Old Mill was used to grind corn and, later, flint. It was known as Heaton Mill and Freeman's Mill at different periods. The present ruins probably date to the early 19th century. However, it is recorded that there was a watermill at this site as far back as 1739, when it was called Mabel's Mill. A corn mill is recorded in the dene as early as the 13th century and was possibly at this location.

For many years from around 1795 and into the 19th century the mill, which produced flour, was owned by the Freeman family. Two of its operators were Paddy or Patrick Freeman (father and son), and one or both of them is commemorated in the name of the park above the eastern bank of the dene. The name of the Freeman Hospital, which stands just across the road from the park is a reminder of the family's long association with the area. As well as milling, they farmed in this area, High Heaton. However, by 1857 the Freemans had vacated the mill and it had been converted to grind flint. The resulting powder was taken to the potteries of the lower Ouseburn.

Another activity took place in the dene; its cliffs and outcrops were quarried for their sandstone. The remains of at least two quarries can still be seen today, one a little to the west of the main waterfall and the other at Blackberry Crag, a little further up river on the eastern side.

Jesmond Dene Mill, 1890.

Also located in Jesmond Dene is the building formerly known as Deep Dene House. This had been the site of a corn watermill, sometimes referred to as Heaton Cottage Mill which was later converted to grind flint for the pottery industry of the lower Ouseburn. In 1861, it was rebuilt or converted into a large residence for Andrew Noble, who became Armstrong's leading deputy at the Elswick Works. However, 10 years later Noble and his family moved to the nearby Jesmond Dene House. Deep Dene House was converted to refreshment rooms in 1900, and eventually became the Fisherman's Lodge restaurant.

After journeying under the imposing Armstrong Bridge, another gift to the city from Lord Armstrong, the waters skirt the western side of the road opposite the Armstrong and Heaton parks. The stream is joined along this stretch by two underground tributaries, the Devil's and Sandyford burns, flowing from the north west. The land for Armstrong Park was a gift from Lord Armstrong in 1879.

Not far from the parks, in the district known as Jesmond Vale, the stream disappears from view into the Ouseburn Culvert. It emerges from this tunnel beneath the Ouseburn rail viaduct, and then journeys under the Metro rail bridge and Byker road bridge, close to Ouseburn Farm. The culvert, built of reinforced concrete, was constructed between 1907 and 1911 to enable the valley to be infilled at this point to provide a crossing place between the centre of Newcastle and Heaton. The infilling took many years and used a large amount of refuse.

A short distance before entering the culvert, the burn passes the site of another flint watermill, which was on its western bank. Located close to Goldspink Lane, it was known as Jesmond Vale Flint Mill and in the early 19th century supplied flint powder to the potteries downstream. Later, it is recorded as producing flour.

Beyond the culvert, the banks of the lower Ouseburn were the main location of Newcastle's pottery and glass industries during the 18th and 19th centuries. Flint and clay carried into the Tyne as ballast by collier ships provided raw materials for the potteries. However, a plentiful and readily available supply of cheap coal was another important factor that led to the establishment of the potteries and glass factories in the area.

One of the first pottery businesses to open in the district was the Low Pottery, which is first mentioned in 1782 but was almost certainly operating earlier. It was located on the eastern bank of the burn. Another pottery was set up at Stepney Bank in around 1786 and this survived in the area, under various owners, until 1912.

The early 19th century witnessed the beginning of the rise of an industrial dynasty in the lower Ouseburn – the Malings. Robert Maling, who moved his business to the valley from Sunderland, founded the Ouseburn Bridge Pottery in around 1815. This establishment was on the eastern bank a little to the south of Ouseburn Bridge. In 1859, his son, Christopher Thompson Maling, set up the nearby Ford Pottery, later known as the Ford A Pottery, also on the eastern bank, and this business was to become one of the most famous of its kind in the area. It stood in what is now the appropriately named Ford Street. Among its numerous products were measuring jugs, mugs and ointment jars.

Maling's expansion continued. In 1879, the company opened the Ford B Pottery at nearby St Lawrence. It was the largest such establishment in the world at the time and covered around 14 acres. The works produced a vast range of products, including countless marmalade and jam jars, tea caddies, tea pots and commemorative items. Both the Ford A and B sites operated in tandem until 1926 when the A Pottery

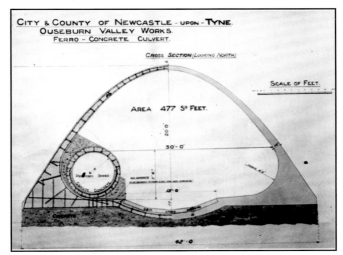

CITY & COUNTY OF NEWCASTLE - UPON - TYNE.
OUSEBURN VALLEY WORKS.
FERRO - CONCRETE CULVERT.

CROSS SECTION (LOOKING NORTH)

SCALE OF FEET.

AREA 477 SQ FEET.

The Ouseburn Culvert:

Clockwise from top left: 1) Construction of the Ouseburn Culvert, 1906. 2) Cross section of the culvert. 3) Workers pose for the camera in 1906. 4) Ouseburn Tip – the rubbish covered culvert snakes away in the distance. 5) The full extent of the culvert revealed in 1907.

closed. The Ford B Pottery continued to operate until 1963. Many of its buildings survive and are still in use as Hoult's Yard, off the eastern end of City Road.

The Ouseburn reaches the Tyne shortly after passing under two bridges. Flanking each side of the penultimate one, the new Glasshouse Bridge, is the Ouseburn Barrage, which is aimed at preventing the water level of the lowest stretch of the Ouseburn from dropping with the tide. The final bridge, at a lower level than its neighbour, marks the approximate site of the stone-built 17th century Glasshouse Bridge, which was demolished in the early 1900s and replaced by the nearby new Glasshouse Bridge.

The old bridge, as its name implies, led to the High, Middle and Low Glasshouses where window glass was manufactured from the 17th century onwards. These works, which also produced other glass products such as mirrors and tumblers, were located to the east of the burn mouth and stretched along the St Lawrence shore towards St Peter's.

The first glass factory in the area was opened by Sir Robert Mansell in around 1619. The site provided easy access to the Tyne for the export of the works' products and the collieries of Tyneside supplied the coal needed to fuel the

A 1906 photograph of the two Glasshouse Bridges taken from the mouth of the Ouseburn. The nearest bridge is the older dating from 1669. The larger bridge dates from 1878. The Ship Inn can be seen between the two bridges. Compare this to the 2014 view on the next page.

fires. Glass-making continued in the lower Ouseburn throughout the 18th and into the 19th century.

One firm survived into the 20th century. This was the bottle-making factory of Liddle Henzell and Company, which continued to operate on the site of the former Ouseburn Bridge Pottery (later the Albion Pottery) until the early 1930s. Coal was delivered to the glass works by wherries (self-propelled barges), which navigated the lowest reaches of the burn.

On the opposite bank to this works stood the Cattle Sanatorium, which housed cattle and sheep imported from Scandinavia. They were kept in quarantine here for 12 hours. Part of this site was later occupied by sweet manufacturers Maynards.

Lead works were another feature of the lower Ouseburn. One of these, the Ouseburn Lead Works, dated to around 1774 and stood on the western bank of the stream a short distance to the north of the Ouseburn rail viaduct. It disappeared as the result of the culverting scheme and infilling of the valley along this stretch.

The scheme also led to the disappearance of a flint mill that stood near Crawford's Bridge, between the rail viaduct and Byker road bridge. This mill seems to have been developed in later years as a pottery.

Close by, the large, impressive building at 36 Lime Street began life in 1848 as a flax mill for the production of linen cloth. In 1866, it was taken over by Procter & Sons, a flour milling business. The year 1896 brought another change of ownership. The building became the premises of York-based millers H. Leetham & Sons. Flour millers Rank were later occupants. Part of the building became the bonded warehouse of wine and spirit merchants J.E. McPherson & Sons, who marketed their Cluny brand of scotch whisky. Today, 36 Lime Street houses art and craft studios and workshops and the well-known Cluny public house and music venue. An adjoining warehouse at 30 Lime Street, also used by the Procter and Leetham milling firms, was built in 1873. Today, it is occupied by Seven Stories, the Centre for Children's Books.

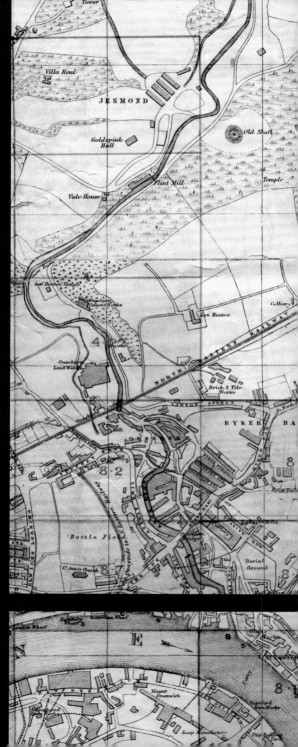

Top: Workers carry out repairs to the wall at Glasshouse Bridge, 30 September 1909.
Right: Section of Bryson's 1865 Plan of Newcastle 'Shewing the Sewerage' Ouseburn Section.
Above: An 1890 photograph of the new Glasshouse Bridge over the Ouseburn.

The Ouseburn barrage keeps the water high in the stream at low tide making the area more attractive.

The development of the Ouseburn area continues with the construction of riverside flats in 2014.

Hidden Burns

The Pandon, Lort and Skinner burns flow underground through central Newcastle, having been culverted and infilled as the result of the many urban developments that have taken place in the city. They now act as rainwater sewers.

The Pandon Burn has its source in the Fountain Row area off Hunters Road, Spital Tongues. From there it flows under Ancrum Street, across Richardson Road and down Owen Court/Framlington Place, between the Castle Leazes and the Town Moor. The burn then journeys alongside the site of Eldon Place, now part of Newcastle University, under Barras Bridge (originally a bridge that spanned the watercourse) and then between Newcastle Civic Centre and St Thomas's Church.

From there, it flows beneath part of Northumbria University and under the East Central Motorway, swinging right past the site of the former New Bridge and then alongside Trafalgar Street, under City Road, beneath the Town Wall remains and then alongside Broad Chare. The stream issues into the Tyne a short distance to the east of the foot of Broad Chare.

The section of the watercourse above Barras Bridge was known as the Bailiff Burn in former times. Barras Bridge is believed to have been named after the barrows (graves) of people who died from leprosy in the Middle Ages and who were cared for at the Hospital of St Mary Magdalene. This hospital stood in the vicinity of St Mary's Place and St Thomas's Church. The cemetery was probably not far from the bridge.

Above right: 1944 Mayoral Christmas greetings featuring Barras Bridge.
Below right: Workers carry out repairs in the Pandon Sewer near Newcastle Civic Centre, October 1986.

The Pandon Burn has a small tributary, the Erick Burn, which has its source approximately between Ridley Place and Northumberland Road. The Erick Burn joins the Pandon Burn to the east of All Saints Church, above the Quayside.

From the vicinity of the grounds of the present-day Civic Centre down to the Tyne, the Pandon Burn formerly ran through a steep-sided dene. However, over a period of many years during the 19th century Pandon Dene shrank in length as it was gradually covered over by urban and railway developments.

Before culverting and infilling, this valley in the midst of a town setting was regarded as a place of great beauty. During the 18th and early 19th centuries it featured small gardens, apple trees and luxuriant foliage. The valley also contained two watermills. New Bridge Street lies along the line of the New Bridge, which was constructed over Pandon Dene in 1812.

The burn takes its name from Pandon, a village adjoining, but originally separate from, Newcastle. However, Pandon, which had been part of the Manor of Byker, was incorporated into Newcastle by permission of Edward I in 1299. The village had the reputation of being an ancient settlement. According to late 18th century historian John Brand, the kings of Northumbria, after the departure of the Romans, were said to have had one of their palaces there.

In 1339, during the reign of Edward III, disaster struck Pandon. The arched opening that allowed the Pandon Burn to flow through the Town Wall became blocked with debris following a long period of incessant rain. The wall acted for a while as a dam, but eventually part of it gave way, leaving a gap of about 100ft, close to Pandon Gate. The resulting torrent of water flooded the Pandon area and '120 laymen, and several priests, besides women' were drowned. Around 140 houses were destroyed.

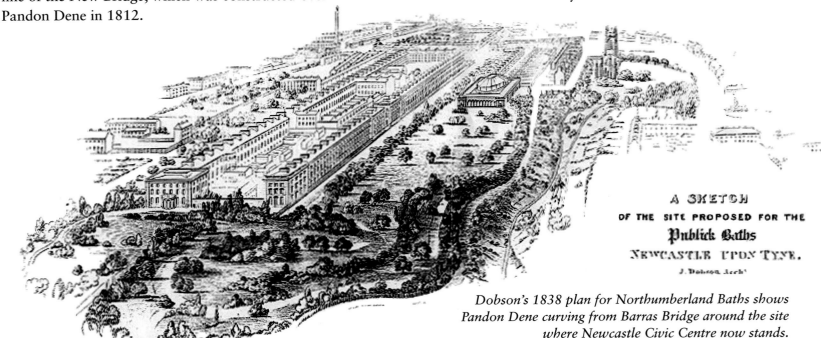

A SKETCH OF THE SITE PROPOSED FOR THE
Publick Baths
NEWCASTLE UPON TYNE.
J. Dobson Arch.

Dobson's 1838 plan for Northumberland Baths shows Pandon Dene curving from Barras Bridge around the site where Newcastle Civic Centre now stands.

An arch that crossed the burn below Pandon Gate was known as Stock Bridge. This crossing was originally made from timber, but about the time of Edward I the Stock Bridge was re-built in stone. Brand states: 'Formerly the river flowed up to it every tide, and there was a fish market near it.' A street known as Stock Bridge later marked the approximate line of the bridge. The name of the crossing may have been taken from the stockfish – fish dried in the open air – which were landed for the market from boats that sailed up the burn, or it could have originated from the early timber bridge. 'Stock' signifies wood.

In December 1294, Edward I ordered that a total of 20 oared galleys, each with a single, square sail, should be built at various ports of the kingdom. War had broken out between England and France in 1293 and Scotland was Edward's enemy. Newcastle was commanded to build one galley. The ship was launched into the Pandon Burn in 1295.

The vessel – more than 100ft in length – was completed the following year. This is the earliest ship recorded to have been constructed on the Tyne and is an indication that Newcastle may have had a shipbuilding industry at this early period.

The source of the Lort Burn can be traced to the Castle Leazes. Culverted for its entire length, it runs into the lake at Leazes Park and then onwards beneath St Thomas Street. Afterwards, the watercourse curves south, across Blackett Street, passing close to the site of the Holy Well of St Batholomew's Nunnery, now covered by the Grainger Market. Near the junction of Grainger and Market Streets it is joined by a tributary, the Lam Burn, which has it source in the Gallowgate area.

The Lort Burn then passes beneath the section of High Bridge between the Bigg Market and Grey Street. From there it flows down the lower part of Grey Street and crosses Mosley Street. The marked dip in the road at the Mosley

Street/Grey Street junction is one of the remaining signs of the stream. It then flows down Dean Street. Near the junction with the Side it is met by a small burn that has its source at Blackfriars. The Lort Burn then passes down the Side, across the Sandhill and into the Tyne near the Guildhall.

Before culverting, the Lort Burn, like the Pandon, ran through a dene. This steep-sided, narrow valley divided Newcastle into western and eastern districts. Two crossings, known as the Upper Dene and Nether Dean bridges, spanned the ravine. The narrow thoroughfare of High Bridge today survives along the approximate line of the upper bridge. It is divided by Grey Street. Likewise, the passage known as Low Bridge, divided by Dean Street, indicates the approximate line of the lower crossing.

The tide flowed up the Lort Burn for a considerable distance, enabling small boats to reach the Nether Dean Bridge (Low Bridge). Bourne states that 'under this very high and ancient arch I am told the rings are still to be seen that the boats were fastened to, which brought up the merchant goods, when the merchants had their shops in the Flesh Market (butchers' market)'. Bourne also writes that 'formerly the river ebbed and flowed above Nether Dean Bridge and boats came under it with wares and commodities for the merchants'.

Far Left: The New Bridge, Pandon Dean c. 1821, by John Lumsden (TWAM). This shows a picturesque view of Pandon Dene, compare this to the modern day bridges and heavy traffic of the now filled in dene (near left).

Above left: Visitors to the Pandon Sewer in grounds of Newcastle Civic Centre, 1975.
Above right: The route of the Pandon Burn between the Civic Centre and St.Mary's Place toward University of Northumbria.
Centre and right: Excavations in 1994 expose the Pandon Burn and Stock Bridge north of the new Law Courts.

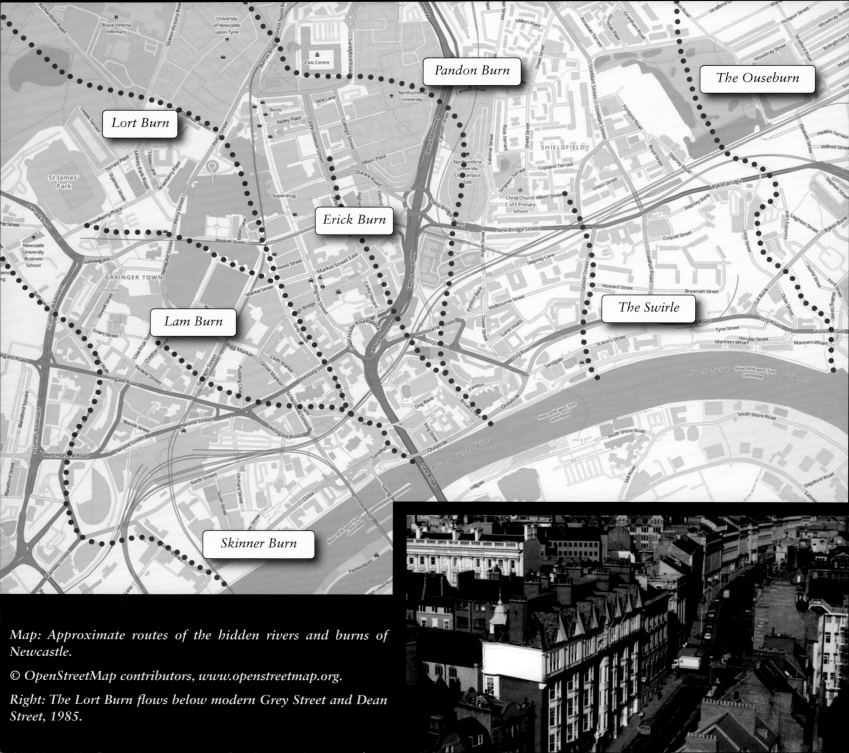

Lort Burn

Pandon Burn

The Ouseburn

Erick Burn

The Swirle

Lam Burn

Skinner Burn

Map: Approximate routes of the hidden rivers and burns of Newcastle.

© OpenStreetMap contributors, www.openstreetmap.org.

Right: The Lort Burn flows below modern Grey Street and Dean Street, 1985.

Clockwise from top left: 1) A metal artwork in Leazes Park celebrates the Lort Burn. 2) The outflow of the Lort Burn near the foot of the Tyne Bridge (1979). 3) A blue plaque showing the location of the 'dirty' Lort Burn. 4) A 1960s inspection of the Lort Burn Sewer somewhere under Grey Street or Dean Street. 5&6) Brick lined sewers beneath Grey Street/Dean Street carry the Lort Burn, part of the High Bridge can still be seen.

At one period another bridge spanned the Lort Burn, approximately at the foot of the Side. There is a story that in 1648 the town's waits (musicians) played on this small bridge to entertain Oliver Cromwell as he ate dinner as the guest of the mayor during a short stay in Newcastle.

In the Middle Ages, a hill or mound of sand was left by the tide near the confluence of the Lort Burn with the Tyne, and this is the origin of the name given to this roughly triangular-shaped area – the Sandhill. It is first recorded in 1310 as a sandy tidal location, frequently flooded.

A market was held here for hundreds of years and the market cross, at the foot of the Side and opposite Sandhill, was known as the Cale Cross. Historian R.J. Charlton in his *Newcastle Town* (1885) states that the cross was mentioned as far back as the reign of Richard II. Bourne declares that it was given its name because of the cale or broth that was sold there. Brand thought it likely that it was named after the herb 'kailwort', which was sold to make the broth.

Whatever the origin of the name, in 1773 the Cale Cross was demolished and 10 years later a new one was erected in its place. However, it was found to be an obstruction to traffic and in 1807 was transferred to the Blagdon Hall estate in Northumberland.

The culverting, infilling and paving of the lowest reach of the Lort Burn, including the Side, had begun by 1646. Work on culverting the Side was complete by 1696. Another stretch of the lower valley was infilled in 1784-1789 as part of the redevelopment of this area of the town by architect David Stephenson. The result was the creation of Dean Street and Mosley Street. The burn had become notorious as a repository for refuse, butchers' offal and effluent of every description and was little more than an open sewer. Indeed, 'lort' was an Anglo-Saxon word for dirt or excrement.

Further culverting and infilling took place higher up the dene during the 1830s when Grey Street, with its magnificent buildings, was created as the result of Richard Grainger's highly impressive redevelopment of the town centre. The Lort Burn now runs beneath part of this elegant and much admired street. During the redevelopment, vast quantities of earth were removed from the Nuns' Fields to infill the dene.

Grainger's redevelopment involved the demolition of the Butcher Market, which had been completed in 1808 and which lay over the Lort Burn. The market was replaced with the new Grainger vegetable and butcher markets between Grainger Street and Newgate Street.

In former years the burn had flowed across the Nuns' Fields and past the large mansion named Anderson Place, originally known as the Newe House, which stood approximately on the site of Lloyds Bank in Grey Street. It was in Anderson Place that Charles I was held prisoner by the Scots during the 17th century. It is claimed that in 1646 Charles tried to escape from his 'house arrest' by fleeing down the Lort Burn on foot. He is said to have come close to reaching a boat waiting at the Quayside to whisk him away, but was captured at the Side.

The Skinner Burn is another underground watercourse that was enclosed in a culvert during the 19th century. It rises near the top end of Bath Lane in the Gallowgate/Pitt Street area.

Bath Lane was built over the burn and was the site of Newcastle's first public baths, which opened in 1781. Cold, tepid and hot baths were provided together with an open-

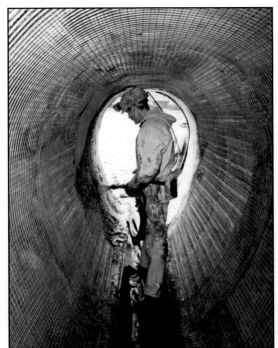

Clockwise from top left: 1) Sandhill in 1920. 2&3) A worker carries out improvement work inside the outflow section of the Skinnerburn below the Queen Elizabeth II Metro Bridge and workers carry out repairs to the Skinnerburn culvert. 4) An etching from around 1780 by W.W. Pybus of the Nether Dene Bridge based on a drawing by T.M. Richardson. Nether Dene Bridge ran between Pilgrim Street and St Nicholas Churchyard.

air swimming pool. Mackenzie declares that 'the situation is remarkably pleasant, in a grove or garden, the walks of which are tastefully fringed with curious shrubs'. However, the water supply for the baths eventually dried up, probably due to the sinking of a nearby pit shaft.

The underground stream passes down Bath Lane, then crosses Westgate Road and journeys under Thornton Square, formerly known as Thornton Street. From there it passes under Waterloo Street and then beneath Marlborough Crescent, the eastern end of Scotswood Road and around the site of the Life Science Centre before dropping down Forth Banks into the Tyne.

The Newcastle Infirmary, which was at the top end of Forth Banks, was founded in 1752. Initially, there were 90 beds but extensions to the hospital meant that by the late 19th century there were 270. It was built on land given by Newcastle Corporation with money subscribed by members of the public. The hospital was also maintained by public subscription. Patients needed a subscriber's letter to be admitted.

The grounds of the Infirmary were laid out with lawns, shrubs, small trees, an ornamental fountain and sculptures. Originally, the Skinner Burn flowed open to the air along the western edge of the hospital grounds but was culverted and topped with infilling to extend the gardens.

N.E.R. FORTH GOODS STATION

Forth Banks in around 1900. The first mention of Parsons' power station was in the local trade directory, Ward's Directory in 1902. The address was listed as 49 and 73 The Close – perhaps the large chimney is associated with the station.

In 1887, the hospital was renamed the Royal Infirmary on the occasion of Queen Victoria's Golden Jubilee. However, it was replaced in 1906 by the new and much larger Royal Victoria Infirmary, built on the Castle Leazes to the north. Today, the site of the old Infirmary is occupied by the Life Science Centre.

At Forth Banks, the Skinner Burn flows under the location of the former Hawthorn Leslie engineering works. The business was begun by Robert Hawthorn, a millwright, in 1817. Robert was joined by his brother William. The firm later began building steam locomotives and marine engines as well as undertaking general engineering work.

In 1872, R.&W. Hawthorn, opened a marine engineering works at St Peter's. The St Peter's Works supplied many of the engines for ships built by Andrew Leslie's yard at Hebburn and it is not surprising that the two firms merged in 1885 to become Hawthorn Leslie.

Backing on to the Hawthorn Leslie Works was the factory established in South Street, off Forth Street, by steam locomotive and railway pioneers George and Robert Stephenson in 1823-25. It was the world's first purpose-built steam locomotive factory. In 1829, this works produced the famous engine *Rocket* for the Liverpool and Manchester Railway. As well as building for the home market, the Stephenson factory, often referred to as the Forth Street Works, exported steam locomotives to numerous countries, including Egypt, Australia, the USA, France, Germany, Norway and Italy.

In 1890, a pioneering electric power station was set up near the foot of Forth Banks to supply power for lighting in the West End of Newcastle. This small station was owned by the Newcastle and District Electric Lighting Company, which had been founded under the leadership of Tyneside-based inventor Charles Parsons in 1889. In the same year, Parsons had set up the Heaton Works, Newcastle, for the manufacture of his steam turbine machinery. Two Parsons' turbo-generators were installed at the Forth Banks power station – the first turbine machinery to be used by any public power station in the world.

One of the smallest of Newcastle's secret burns is the Swirle. This tiny watercourse in the Sandgate district flows into the Tyne. It was culverted in the 19th century.

Brand states that the Swirle was originally known as 'The Squirrel.' Perhaps this was an allusion to the fast-flowing, lively nature of the burn's waters.

The Swirle formed part of Newcastle's eastern boundary until 1549. In that year the boundary was moved eastwards to the St Lawrence district, creating an area where ballast from ships could be deposited. This no doubt strengthened the town's control over collecting ballast charges.

Today, a short street near the Pitcher and Piano bar on the Quayside has been named The Swirle and this is on the approximate line of the diminutive stream. An impressive artwork/architectural structure nearby is named the Swirle Pavilion. The work, by Raf Fulcher, commemorates the shipping and trading connections of the Tyne with ports in Britain and on the Continent of Europe.

The source of the Swirle can be traced to the Clarence Street area of Shieldfield. The burn flows under New Bridge Street, Gibson Street, City Road, across Sandgate and along the modern-day street named The Swirle.

Top: The Swirle in 1926. Right: Work is stopped in 1969 when workers rediscover the route of The Swirle. Middle: Modern street signs reflect the past (note the Tyne God detail). Bottom: Modern offices and the artwork Swirle Pavilion by Raf Fulcher mark the course of the hidden stream.

Streams celebrated

Five artworks celebrate hidden burns of Newcastle.

1. The course of the Lort Burn down the Side is marked by an artwork entitled *Tributary*. This includes granite paving with slate laid in the street in such a way as to represent the downward flow of the burn towards the Tyne. There are radial slabs of slate where the road merges with the Sandhill opposite the Guildhall. The artwork is by John Maine, RA.

2. A sculpture, *Give and Take*, is sited above the course of the Pandon Burn in Trinity Gardens at the top of Broad Chare. The work, by Peter Randall-Page, is formed from a large glacial boulder found in Scotland. The artist has carved hexagons and pentagons into the surface of the boulder, symbolising the microscopic structures found in nature. The base of the sculpture features a pattern of cobbles that represents the river bed of the hidden stream. The title of the work indicates the balance between order and chaos that the work illustrates.

3. An artwork that celebrates the Lort Burn can be found in Leazes Park. The extensive multi-part work, by Tom Grimsey, is entitled *The Flowering of the Lort Burn*. It consists of blue terrazzo slabs and plants representing the stream. The terrazzo is inset with colourful ceramic and metal flowers. They mark the line of the Lort Burn. Metal flowers are also set into paths above the burn and a railing in the form of waves marks the place where the burn enters the lake. At the north end of the park, near the source of the watercourse, there is a splash pool, with sculptural seating and play structures.

4. The Skinner Burn is celebrated with *Tyne Line of Txt Flow* by Carol Sommer, Sue Downing and W.N. Herbert. The work, in Thornton Square (formerly known as Thornton Street), takes the form of words on a metal strip set between paving stones. The strip flows over public seating as well as the surface of the square. The text is taken from Roman messages discovered in the North East, words printed during the reign of King Charles I and text messages from the day of a Newcastle United v Sunderland football match. The work marks the course of the Skinner Burn.

5. *Pillar Man* is a bronze sculpture in front of the outer wall of Northumbria University Gallery. The tall figure of a man emerges from a dark granite 'stream' that is sited above the course of the Pandon Burn. The sculpture is by Nicolaus Widerberg. The granite river has been polished to represent water.

1. Tributary

2. Give and Take

3. The Flowering of the Lort Burn

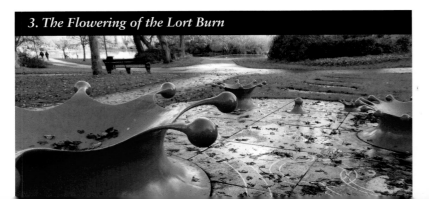

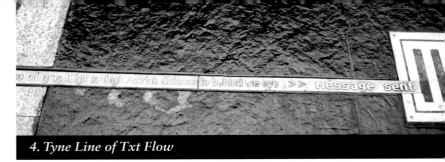

to bring us thigh to thigh / shrink distance to behind the eye >> message sent

4. Tyne Line of Txt Flow

5. Pillar Man

Above: Workers on Glasshouse Bridge, 18 January 1908.
Right: Inspection of the Pandon Sewer near its outfall into the
Tyne, 24th March 1977. The stone work in the top picture suggests
an old bridge buried beneath modern streets.